MW01098907

GLOBAL CITIZENSHIP

Making Global Connections

SUSAN WATSON

This edition first published in 2004 in the United States of America by Smart Apple Media.

All rights reserved. No part of this book may be reproduced in any form or by any means without written permission from the publisher.

Smart Apple Media
1980 Lookout Drive
North Mankato
Minnesota 56003

Library of Congress Cataloging-in-Publication Data

Watson, Susan, 1949–
    Making global connections / by Susan Watson.
    p. cm — (Global citizenship)

    Summary: Describes the way in which international communication, migration, sports, business, politics, and aid make us all citizens of the whole world.

    ISBN 1-58340-405-8
    1. International relations—Juvenile literature. 2. Communication, International—Juvenile literature. 3. World citizenship—Juvenile literature. 4. Globalization—Juvenile literature. [1. International relations. 2. Communication, International. 3. World citizenship. 4. Globalization.] I. Title.
    JZ1305.W38 2003
    3033.48'2—dc21   2002044628

First Edition
9 8 7 6 5 4 3 2 1

First published in 2003 by
MACMILLAN EDUCATION AUSTRALIA PTY LTD
627 Chapel Street, South Yarra, Australia 3141

Associated companies and representatives throughout the world.

Copyright © Susan Watson 2003

Packaged for Macmillan Education Australia by Publishing Options Pty Ltd
Text design by Gail McManus Graphics
Cover design by Dimitrios Frangoulis
Illustrations by Infographics Pty Ltd
Page make-up by Crackerjack Desktop Services

Printed in Thailand

Acknowledgements

The author is especially grateful to Matthew, Kyja, CJ, and Samantha for being the model global citizens of this series. The author and the publisher would like to thank the following for permission to reproduce copyright materials:

Cover photograph: United Nations National Assembly, courtesy of Australian Picture Library/Corbis.

AAP/AP Photo/Brennan Linsley, p. 22 (bottom); ANT Photo Library, pp. 22–3 (center); AusAID, p. 26 (top); Jean-Paul Ferrero/Auscape International, p. 24; Australian Picture Library/Corbis, pp. 14, 19; logo used with permission of the Australian Red Cross, p. 29; Coo-ee Picture Library, pp. 9, 11 (top); screendump used with permission of the Fair Trade Foundation, p. 17; Getty Images, pp. 4–5 (center), 6, 7, 12, 15 (top), 28 (top right); © 2002 Mark A. Johnson, p. 10 (left); screendump used with permission of OneWorld, p. 27; Brian Parker, pp. 16, 29 (bottom); logo used with permission of the Rainforest Action Network, p. 28; Reuters, pp. 13, 20; logo used with permission of UNESCO, p. 19; logo used with permission of UNICEF, p. 19; Susan Watson, pp. 4 (far left), 4 (center left), 5 (center right), 5 (far right), 30; World Vision, p. 25; logo used with permission of World Wide Fund For Nature, p. 28; screendump used with permission of the Youth Sustainable Consumption Program of UNEP (United Nations Environment Programme), p. 21.

While every care has been taken to trace and acknowledge copyright, the publisher tenders their apologies for any accidental infringement where copyright has proved untraceable. Where the attempt has been unsuccessful, the publisher welcomes information that would redress the situation.

Please note

At the time of printing, the Internet addresses appearing in this book were correct. Owing to the dynamic nature of the Internet, however, we cannot guarantee that all these addresses will remain correct.

Contents

Global citizens

A global citizen is a person who:
◎ has rights and responsibilities
◎ acts in a caring way based on knowledge and understanding
◎ relates to others within their family, friendship groups, community, and country
◎ develops personal values and commitments
◎ develops a sense of their own role in the world.

A study of global citizenship will help you understand how people affect the quality of global environments and the well-being of others. Active global citizens do not just sit back and wait for others to do something. They turn their ideas into action. Action can take many forms:
◎ volunteering by giving time, help, and ideas freely
◎ talking to your friends
◎ thinking deeply
◎ learning more
◎ taking part in community events.

Throughout this book Allira, Harry, Lin, and Denzel will tell you their ways of acting as global citizens. We can all care for each other and our environment.

citizen
a person living in a larger group of people who they mix with

environments
natural and built surroundings

ALLIRA

Hi! I'm Allira. I live in a large country town near the sea. My family background is Aboriginal–Australian.

HARRY

Hello. I'm Harry. I live with my family in a suburb of a big modern city of four million people.

we are global citizens

Global citizens connect globally

A global citizen is a person who mixes with people and cultures from around the world. We all live within our own family and community groups. We all live within local and national political borders. However, there are ways that we can go beyond these to make global connections. We can:

◎ contact people all over the world by phone, e-mail, and the Internet
◎ travel to other countries
◎ watch world events unfold on television
◎ buy things that are made in other places.

Today, there are many large businesses whose influence spreads across the globe. There are also organizations that operate at the international level to help people improve the quality of their lives. There are international laws and agreements that join countries together on important global issues, such as:

◎ to protect the environment
◎ to protect human rights
◎ for trade
◎ for defense.

These global connections can help people work towards a fairer and more sustainable world.

international
worldwide

trade
the buying and selling of goods and services between different places

We are global citizens

LIN

I'm Lin. I migrated to my new country with my parents. We live with my grandparents who came 15 years ago from Malaysia.

DENZEL

Hi! I'm Denzel. My mom and I live in a high-rise apartment close to the city center. We're African-American.

Young people connect to each other all over the world.

Transportation

Most people use some form of transportation in their daily lives. People use transportation to connect with other people in their community, with places further away in their own country, and with countries outside their own.

The first form of transportation technology to connect people globally was the sailing ship. From the 1500s onwards, ships transported people and goods across the world's oceans. By the early 1900s, large numbers of people started using other transportation to go to different countries. First, this was by train, then in cars and buses, and then by airplane.

technology
modern equipment and processes

Super-highways

Today people can make country-to-country connections in the comfort of their own car or a tour bus. Modern roads move millions of tons of goods and thousands of people across countries every day. There is a complex system of roads in many countries. Super-highways now make road transportation even easier.

GLOBAL FACT
The fastest passenger jet is the Concorde, which cruises at more than 1,305 miles (2,100 km) per hour. It takes passengers from London to New York in 3.5 hours.

Airlines

About 50 years ago, passenger airplanes started moving large numbers of people around the globe. Today, it is possible to be in another place, more than halfway round the world in less than a day. Airline travel has become cheaper in the last 20 years. More and more people are making business and cultural connections using air travel.

Air travel makes it easy for people to connect globally.

Media networks

Millions of people connect to the world every day through the media—newspapers, TV, and radio. There has been a big growth in the number of TV news, current affairs, and documentary programs. TV is the world's most powerful means of communication. When a major event happens anywhere in the world, people can watch it unfolding from their living rooms. It is estimated that about one billion people watched the attack on the World Trade Center in New York on September 11, 2001.

The media also brings the world's entertainers into our homes.

digital divide
the gap between people who use computers and those who do not

Digital technology

Digital technology is computer-based technology. Computers have been around in business since the 1960s and personal computers since the 1980s. Mobile phones and satellites are also part of digital technology.

The Internet is a global network connecting millions of computers in more than 100 countries. People connect almost instantly to each other to swap data, news, and opinions through e-mail and Web pages. This form of digital technology only became widely available in the mid 1990s.

However, at the start of 2002, no more than 10 percent of the world's population had access to the Internet. Many countries and people suffer from the digital divide.

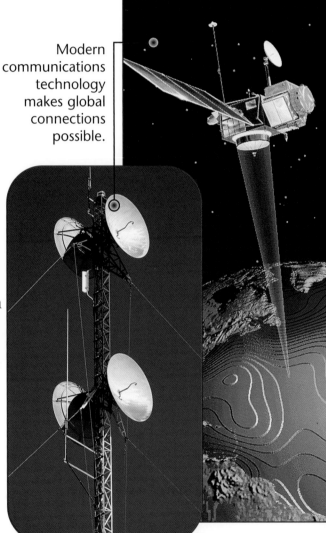

Modern communications technology makes global connections possible.

Super-highways make it easy for people and goods to connect across a number of countries.

What can I do?

I'm going to ask our teacher if we can use the Internet to connect to a class in another country. Somewhere in Finland or Canada would be cool. We can find out their different names, what their families are like, what things they celebrate, and what it's like where they live.

International migration

People have been on the move for thousands of years. Many have traveled from one place to live in another. They have been part of different waves of migration across the world. People become migrants for different reasons such as, to:

◎ find work and better living conditions
◎ join other family members already living in a new country
◎ escape war or a natural disaster
◎ find freedom and peace
◎ experience adventure and exploration.

A multicultural world

cultural diversity the variety of cultural backgrounds in the world's people

Countries like the United States, Canada, the United Kingdom, Australia, and Germany have taken in migrants for more than 100 years. Migrants have been important in taking jobs in factories and helping the economies of the countries grow. Some migrants with farming backgrounds started farms and others started businesses in their new countries. Others, with qualifications, work in different professions.

Countries with groups of migrant people become multicultural societies. People are encouraged to practice their customs and traditions, provided that they are within the country's laws. In a multicultural society, people from a range of backgrounds make global connections through cultural diversity.

Many of the world's people have moved from country to country in waves of migration at different times.

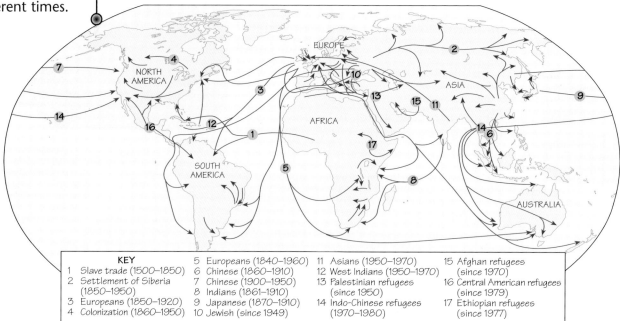

KEY
1 Slave trade (1500–1850)
2 Settlement of Siberia (1850–1950)
3 Europeans (1850–1920)
4 Colonization (1860–1950)
5 Europeans (1840–1960)
6 Chinese (1860–1910)
7 Chinese (1900–1950)
8 Indians (1861–1910)
9 Japanese (1870–1910)
10 Jewish (since 1949)
11 Asians (1950–1970)
12 West Indians (1950–1970)
13 Palestinian refugees (since 1950)
14 Indo-Chinese refugees (1970–1980)
15 Afghan refugees (since 1970)
16 Central American refugees (since 1979)
17 Ethiopian refugees (since 1977)

New citizenship

Global connections are made stronger when people who have migrated decide to become citizens of their new country. Migrants can do this once they have lived in the new country for a certain period of time. They must also fit in with the standards for citizenship set by the country.

Some countries ask migrants to give up the nationality of their birthplace when becoming a citizen of their new homeland. Other countries allow people to hold dual citizenship. This means they have two sets of the rights and responsibilities that come with being a citizen. A person who migrates from Tonga to New Zealand, is allowed to be a citizen of both countries.

It is even possible to hold multiple citizenships. Someone who lives in a country that has very close ties with a number of other countries can often be a "citizen" of the other countries. Citizens of any of the 15 member countries of the European Union (EU) are able to connect easily.

citizenship
becoming a citizen of a country by being accepted into its nationality

European Union (EU)
a group of 15 countries in Europe who have joined together for economic reasons

People who migrate can become citizens of their new country in a formal citizenship ceremony held by government officials.

CASE STUDY: Irish citizens hold multiple citizenship

Ireland is a country in Western Europe, across a sea channel from Wales and England. Irish law allows dual citizenship and does not ask migrants to give up their birth nationality. In fact, Irish citizens have multiple citizenships.

Ireland is a member of the European Union. Irish citizens are also citizens of the European Union. They are allowed to live and work in any of the EU member nations:

- **Austria**
- **Finland**
- **Greece**
- **Luxembourg**
- **Spain**
- **Belgium**
- **France**
- **Ireland**
- **Netherlands**
- **Sweden**
- **Denmark**
- **Germany**
- **Italy**
- **Portugal**
- **United Kingdom.**

GLOBAL FACT
There are over 70 million people throughout the world who are of Irish descent and 40 million of these are U.S. citizens.

International travel

Traveling to another place as a tourist is a way of connecting to other people around the globe. Tourism used to be a luxury that only rich people could afford. However, in the last 50 years, transportation by road, railroad, air, and sea has become faster and more comfortable. Travel has also become cheaper so more and more people are traveling. Many go to foreign countries. They are international tourists.

There are different reasons why people travel:

◎ for pleasure and relaxation
◎ for adventure and excitement
◎ to escape from routine
◎ for sporting activities
◎ to do something different
◎ for education
◎ to visit relatives
◎ for work and business
◎ to experience other cultures
◎ for religious reasons.

developing countries countries with much lower standards of wealth and comfort than developed countries

Tourism creates a lot of jobs for people. More than 10 percent of all the jobs in the world are related to travel in some way. Tourism is an important part of the economy of most countries. Many developing countries rely on tourism to help provide jobs and help their economies grow.

International tourists experience cultures outside of their own because travel helps them make global connections.

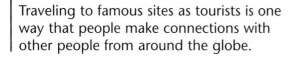

Traveling to famous sites as tourists is one way that people make connections with other people from around the globe.

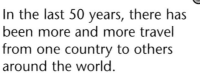

In the last 50 years, there has been more and more travel from one country to others around the world.

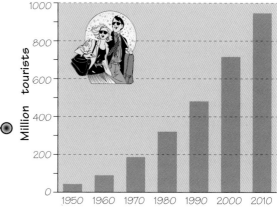

Ecotourists are global citizens

A special form of tourism has developed around the world's natural and cultural heritage. Ecotourism is tourist activities that are done in harmony with the natural environment. Ecotourists also respect and value the cultural backgrounds of indigenous peoples.

When ecotourists make global connections they can:

◎ experience the diversity of life on Earth
◎ learn about the threats to global environments
◎ be taught by indigenous peoples who have important local knowledge
◎ help the economies of the developing countries where many ecotourism activities are located.

Ecotourists who travel to developing countries often return home with real concern for those countries. Their global connections help them become caring global citizens. Ecotourists aim to keep the planet sustainable.

heritage
things from the past and present that are valued and saved for future generations

harmony
with a sense of balance

indigenous peoples
groups with the same language and culture who are related to the first people in an area

sustainable
to stay strong and last for a long period of time

Ecotourists view ancient rock art while protecting the natural environment by walking on boardwalks.

What can I do?

A family friend of ours works as a park ranger in Kakadu National Park in northern Australia. She is one of the indigenous owners of the land. She's also part of the ecotourism team there and has lots of local knowledge about the environment. I'm going to ask her what she tells the ecotourists about Aboriginal people's connection to their land.

The Olympic Games

Sports are another way that people make global connections. Sporting connections have been helped by faster transportation and also by the world media. The media covers major events and millions of people around the globe can see or hear them.

The Olympic Games began more than two thousand years ago in Ancient Greece. It brought warring groups together for a peaceful celebration. Today, the Olympic Games is a peaceful competition for the world's greatest athletes. It is a global sporting event, held every four years, that draws people together. It gives competitors and spectators from around the world the chance of connecting in a spirit of friendly competition.

The symbols of the Olympic Games show this spirit:
◎ the plain white background of the Olympic flag stands for peace throughout the games
◎ the Olympic flame stands for purity, the aim of perfection, the struggle for victory, and also peace and friendship.

The Para-Olympics for disabled people is an event that follows the Olympic Games. It also draws people together worldwide. The Para-Olympics helps people appreciate the diversity in athletes who want to compete in world events.

The Olympic Games brings competitors together from nearly every country and attracts the interest of millions of spectators around the globe.

World competition events

Every year, there are world events in single sports that bring people together from around the globe. There is usually strong media coverage of these events provided to a world of spectators.

Soccer has the largest following of all global sports. Internationally, it is called "football." The soccer World Cup final takes place every four years after competitions in all regions of the globe. There are also world cup and world championship events in other sports. Some special events, although not called "world" events, attract international competitors and millions of media spectators.

World sporting competition is a way that global citizens connect to become more aware of the world they live in.

GLOBAL FACT

Only 15 countries did not compete in the 2002 World Cup in soccer.

World Cup	World championship	International event
Soccer	Superbikes	Boston Marathon
Skateboarding	Netball	British Open Golf
Triathlon	Swimming	Formula 1 Grand Prix
Cricket	Athletics	Rip Curl Surfing
Skiing	Wheelchair rugby	The Melbourne Cup horse race
Marathon swimming	Chess	Tennis Grand Slam

The Para-Olympic Games connects the world's disabled athletes as well as millions of spectators.

What can I do?

The Tour de France is this great cycling race that happens over three weeks every July. I'm going to follow it on TV and learn about all the different competitors and teams. It'd be so cool if an American wins it again!

Globalization

Modern transportation and digital technologies have helped businesses spread all over the world. Big business companies in developed countries such as the U.S., Germany, the United Kingdom, and Japan now have factories in developing countries such as India, Mexico, South Africa, and Thailand. Labor is cheaper in developing countries and huge container ships make it easy to transport goods anywhere.

Motor-vehicle and gasoline companies

Some of the largest transnationals (known as TNCs) are motor-vehicle companies. General Motors (the U.S.) is the world's largest corporation. In 1999, there were only 22 countries out of the world's 195 that made more money than General Motors. Other huge motor-vehicle companies are the Ford Motor Company (the U.S.), Daimler-Chrysler (Germany), Toyota (Japan), and Volkswagen (Germany). All these TNCs have factories in various regions of the world.

A few huge oil TNCs have also spread throughout the world. Three companies supply most of the world's countries with oil and petrol. These are Exxon–Mobil (the U.S.), Royal Dutch Shell (Netherlands/United Kingdom), and BP Amoco (United Kingdom).

Some global citizens feel that there could be problems when so few TNCs seem to control cars and gasoline. Cars burn gasoline and oil, and add to greenhouse gases, but changing to environmentally friendly cars and fuel is costly.

developed countries
countries with a high standard of wealth and comforts for most people

transnationals (TNCs)
huge business companies that have a head office in one country and factories in other countries

greenhouse gases
the gases that surround Earth and trap heat near the surface

GLOBAL FACT
There are 10 motor-vehicle and oil companies in the world's 20 largest TNCs.

The world's large oil and petroleum companies have outlets in every country.

Fast-food chains

Thirty years ago most of the fast food that was eaten was in the U.S., Canada, England, and a few other countries like Australia. Today, hundreds of millions of people around the world buy fast food. Whether they are in Sydney, Los Angeles, Beijing, or Capetown, they stand in line to order from a photo-display menu, find a seat at a table, unwrap the paper, and start eating.

There are now hundreds of thousands of fast-food outlets worldwide. Most of these have come from American food chains such as McDonald's, KFC, Pizza Hut, Wendy's, and Burger King. McDonald's and KFC make half their profit from overseas outlets. McDonald's opens almost 2,000 new stores each year. It has replaced Coca-Cola as the world's most famous brand.

GLOBAL FACT

In 1968, McDonald's operated about 1,000 restaurants. Today, it has over 30,000 restaurants worldwide.

Clothing and footwear companies

A baseball cap worn backwards, a brand-name T-shirt, a pair of blue jeans, thick socks, and a pair of sneakers. This is the everyday dress for many of the world's young city people. Brand-name clothes and shoes such as Nike, Puma, Adidas, Levis, and Doc Martens are likely to have been made in a developing country. Large clothing and footwear TNCs operate factories in Asia and South America, in particular. Many of these corporations now only have a head office in a developed country, with their manufacturing plants in a foreign location.

Many well-known brands started in the U.S. Today, they are found in many different countries with different cultures.

What can I do?

I'm going to read the labels on my clothes and shoes, and the food we buy at the supermarket. I'll get to know which different countries they're made in. I'll think about how globalization of business could be both good and bad for the world.

World trade

wealth
the amount of money and resources that a country has

tariffs
extra costs or taxes put on imports from another country, making them more expensive

Most countries in the world cannot produce all of the goods and services that their populations need or want so they trade. Trade between countries is very old. Countries also trade because some things could be cheaper to buy from other countries than making them. Trade is a two-way process because things come into and go out of countries.

◎ A country imports when it buys goods and services from other countries.

◎ A country exports when it sells goods and services to other countries.

Countries export to try to become wealthier. Wealth is important for all countries, especially developing countries. If it is used fairly, wealth from trade can help reduce poverty and create more jobs.

Trade helps countries make global connections with other countries. Global connections can lead to better understanding between trading countries.

World Trade Organization

The United Nations set up the World Trade Organization (WTO) in 1995. The main aim of the WTO is to have a better sharing of world trade for all countries, not just the powerful ones like the U.S., Japan, and those in the European Union. More than 130 nations are members of the WTO.

Some countries of the world put tariffs on the imports that are bought in from other countries. Governments use tariffs to try to protect goods and services in their own country. The WTO wants to make countries of the world trade freely. The WTO wants governments to allow free movement of goods and services without tariffs.

The world's oceans have thousands of large container ships like this that travel between countries carrying items for trade.

Effects of globalization

In today's business world, the number of transnational corporations (TNCs) is getting fewer. Big TNCs are joining with other big TNCs to make even bigger TNCs. This has the result that world business and trade is controlled by huge TNCs that have a lot of power. They can often put pressure on governments for their own interests. However, the interests of big business are not always the same as the interests of local people.

Even where factories have been set up in developing countries, TNCs can control the working conditions and rates of pay. Working conditions are often poor compared to developed countries, with low wages, poor health and safety, and no job security into the future.

Another concern about globalization of business is that it can destroy cultural diversity. This is because people all over the world seem to be changing their traditional customs. They want to eat fast food, wear the latest fashions, and buy the latest pop music from countries such as the U.S. and the United Kingdom.

Global citizens can help by being concerned about fair trade and working conditions in other countries.

GLOBAL FACT

Part of the world's supply of cocoa, which makes chocolate, is harvested by child slaves in Ivory Coast, West Africa. This helps chocolate-makers keep prices down.

slaves
people who are owned by another, have no freedom, and must obey the owner

Yennadon School
Library

CASE STUDY — Making trade fairer for all

The Fair Trade Foundation started in London to help the world's developing countries get a better deal from world trade. The Foundation has a brand called the Fairtrade Mark. This trademark lets consumers know that the products have been produced fairly and that the proper price has been paid for them. The trademark also means that workers making the products had decent working conditions.

Consumers can start making a difference by buying things marked with the Fairtrade Mark. It is used on the packaging of teas, coffees, chocolates, honey, and other products.

The Web site of the Fair Trade Foundation reports on current issues and displays the Fairtrade Mark logo.

Global political connections

International government organizations

There are around 300 international organizations in the world today. They work for the combined benefit of a group of countries that form an international government organization (IGO). The countries in the IGO act together for particular reasons, such as trade or defense. An IGO can have a few member countries or many.

IGOs	Member countries and reason for cooperation
APEC (Asia–Pacific Economic Community)	21 member nations that make trade agreements between themselves—Australia, Brunei Darussalam, Canada, Chile, China, Hong Kong (China), Chinese Taipei, Indonesia, Japan, Republic of Korea, Malaysia, Mexico, New Zealand, Papua New Guinea, Peru, Philippines, Russia, Singapore, Thailand, the U.S., Vietnam
NAFTA (North American	3 member nations that cooperate on trade—the U.S., Canada, and Mexico
The EU (the European Union)	15 members nations that cooperate for economic reasons and have a common money, the Euro-dollar—Austria, Belgium, Denmark, Finland, France, Germany, Greece, Ireland, Italy, Luxembourg, Netherlands, Portugal, Spain, Sweden, United Kingdom
NATO (North Atlantic Treaty Organization)	19 member nations; 17 are European nations who have joined with the U.S. and Canada for defense reasons—Belgium, Czech Republic, Denmark, France, Germany, Greece, Hungary, Iceland, Italy, Luxembourg, Netherlands, Norway, Poland, Portugal, Spain, Turkey, United Kingdom

The United Nations

The United Nations (UN) is the world's largest IGO. It was started at the end of World War II in 1945 to help keep peace in the world. Many countries are members of it.

The United Nations is concerned for all people in all countries. It tries to develop friendly relations among nations by making global connections between them. It works for international cooperation in helping to solve economic, human, and environmental problems.

GLOBAL FACT

In the year 2002, there were 191 member nations of the United Nations.

Most of the countries of the world have representatives who meet in the United Nations General Assembly in New York. This is where important decisions are made in world politics.

UN agencies

The UN is responsible for coordinating the work of over 60 different agencies that operate throughout the world. Different UN agencies help look after the interests of the world's heritage, children, and developing countries. The agencies try to find solutions to global issues.

agencies
subgroups of a large organization

UNICEF is the United Nations Children's Fund. It has its headquarters in New York City. UNICEF carries out its work through more than 160 countries, territories, and areas. It tries to reduce childhood death and illness and to protect children during war and natural disaster.

The World Bank is a group of five large organizations that manage money and issues related to economic development. The main aim is to reduce poverty in the world.

The ILO is the International Labor Organization. It recommends basic standards of work and labor rights for all the world's workers. The ILO is concerned about unfair treatment of workers. It has a special campaign against child labor, where children are forced to work in very poor conditions at a young age.

UNESCO is the United Nations Educational, Scientific, and Cultural Organization. It has its headquarters in Paris, France, and 56 field offices and units in different parts of the world. UNESCO aims to help peace and security in the world through education, science, culture, and communication. UNESCO is responsible for the World Heritage List.

United Nations Educational, Scientific and Cultural Organization.

World peacekeeping

conflict
violent
disagreement

civilian
a person who does
not belong to any
defense forces

War and conflict occur regularly in different parts of the world. Since 1948, the United Nations has organized special groups of people to manage troublespots when a conflict ends. These are UN Peacekeeping Forces. They help put peace agreements into action, check that ceasefires are obeyed, and help with rebuilding the war-torn area.

UN Peacekeeping Forces wear blue helmets or blue berets so they can be easily recognized. The forces are made up of:
◎ military troops
◎ civilian police officers.
Other civilians often help, too. They give special help in watching elections take place and in checking if there have been abuses of human rights.

Since 1948, there have been 54 UN peacekeeping operations. Forty-one of those operations have been since 1990. There are currently 12 UN peacekeeping operations around the world.

The UN has no army or police of its own. It calls on member nations to provide troops and equipment. Civilians often volunteer. Some are paid by organizations that want to help the peace process. The people involved in peacekeeping make global connections and act as citizens for peace.

GLOBAL FACT

More than 1,650 UN military and civilian peacekeepers have died in the performance of their duties since 1948.

UN peacekeeping operations

Africa	Period
Western Sahara	April, 1991–present
Sierra Leone	October, 1999–present
Democratic Republic of the Congo	November, 1999–present
Ethiopia and Eritrea	July, 2000–present
Middle East	
Middle East	June, 1948–present
Golan Heights	June, 1974–present
Lebanon	March, 1978–present
Asia	
India/Pakistan	January, 1949–present
East Timor	October, 1999–present
Europe	
Cyprus	March, 1964–present
Georgia	August, 1993–present
Kosovo	June, 1999–present

UN Peacekeeping Forces operate in places where conflicts have occurred.

World youth and the environment

Youths aged between 16 and 25 years make up nearly 30 percent of the world's population. The way that young people consume today will influence what they want in their adult lifestyles. The United Nations understands the importance of the role young people play in the protection of the environment. In 1999, the United Nations Environment Programme (UNEP) started to work with young people on ideas about how to reduce the amount people consume.

Youths from 17 countries on five continents are making global connections through UNEP's Youth and Sustainable Consumption Campaign. Sustainable consumption is a similar ideal to ecologically sustainable development (ESD). Groups of young people are telling UNEP about how they live and what resources they use in their own countries.

UNEP also made a survey that was given to 15,000 young people in 25 countries. It asked them what they knew about the impact their lifestyles and consumption had on the environment, economy, and society. The results showed that young people are most concerned about the pollution of the air, water, and soil, then health, human rights, and population issues. Young people can be global citizens who care about global issues.

consume
to buy things and use them in everyday living

ecologically sustainable development (ESD)
living in a way that reduces human impact on Earth and helps preserve resources for the future

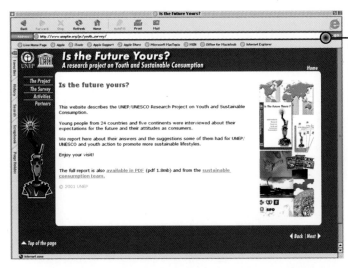

The United Nations is helping young people around the world connect in the Sustainable Consumption Campaign being run by its Environment Program.

What can I do?

My big sister is 17. She's part of a group that keeps in touch over the Internet about the Sustainable Consumption Campaign. I'm going to ask her what ideas they've come up with for reducing global consumption.

International agreements

One of the main ways that countries connect about issues of global concern is through a treaty. Representatives of the countries usually meet to sign the treaty in a formal ceremony to show how important it is.

A similar form of international agreement is called a convention. Conventions are general rules of behavior on issues. International conventions become general practice for many of the world's countries.

International agreements help find solutions to important global issues.

treaty
an agreement between two or more countries, which they all sign

environmental issues
problems that are about the environment

humanitarian issues
problems that are about human lives

landmines
bombs hidden in the earth that explode when stepped on

Environmental issues

There are many global environmental issues. When countries are concerned about these they join together to try to solve them. For example, there is an international environmental agreement that connects countries in their efforts to save whales. Whales are protected under the "Convention on International Trade in Endangered Species of Wild Fauna and Flora," which 144 countries have signed.

Whales are protected under an international convention.

Humanitarian issues

There are many global humanitarian issues. Some people live in places that do not allow them to have their full human rights. For example, war harms people's human rights. Many countries are concerned about the problems of landmines.

GLOBAL FACT

More than 60 countries have signed the "International Treaty to Ban Landmines."

Landmines cause damage to civilian people, even long after a war has ended.

Agreements about global warming

Many of the world's scientists and other experts agree that global warming is one of the biggest environmental issues now facing planet Earth. They think that higher amounts of greenhouse gases in our atmosphere cause global warming.

Developed countries produce a high level of greenhouse gas emissions per person because of the number of factories and motor vehicles. Greenhouse gas emissions are less in developing countries than in developed countries. However, these could increase as developing countries build more factories and use more motor vehicles.

There is an international agreement about controlling global warming called the Kyoto Protocol.

global warming an overall increase in the world's temperature

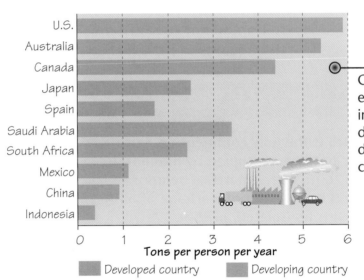

Greenhouse emissions in some developed and developing countries.

Tons per person per year

Developed country   Developing country

CASE STUDY — The Kyoto Protocol on Greenhouse Emissions

In 1997, the United Nations organized a meeting in Kyoto, Japan about global warming. The environment ministers from 159 countries met to discuss the effect of higher levels of greenhouse gases in the atmosphere. Most agreed that more greenhouse gases cause global warming and that action was needed to reduce them. The countries agreed to a convention called the Kyoto Protocol that would try to get the world to limit greenhouse gas emissions.

Part of the agreement was to get countries to stop their factories, motor vehicles, and farm animals from putting so much carbon dioxide and methane back into the air. They set targets for each country and agreed to meet these by 2012.

Since then, a UN organization called the Conference of the Parties (COP) has met every year to check on the progress of the convention.

Agreements about the polar lands

Not many people have been to the polar lands near the north pole in the Arctic and the south pole in Antarctica. The polar environment is harsh and deserted, but it is still one of the global environments that need protecting and preserving. Polar lands are the last pristine areas on Earth.

pristine
totally unspoiled by humans

exploit
to use selfishly and for personal gain

There are many species of plant and animal life found in polar regions that do not exist anywhere else. In the Arctic National Wildlife Refuge in Alaska, the rich diversity of wildlife includes more than 160 bird species, 36 kinds of land mammals, 9 marine mammal species, and 36 types of fish. Antarctica also has a huge diversity of plant and animal life.

The polar lands are also rich in oil and minerals, which some countries want to exploit. Their protection is a global environmental issue. There are international agreements to protect polar regions as part of the world's natural heritage.

CASE STUDY   The Antarctic Treaty

Antarctica is the only continent on Earth that has not been occupied by humans. It belongs to no one. Antarctica belongs to itself, and it is a common heritage of all people. It is an isolated, pristine environment.

Many nations have made claims to Antarctica but they have only been allowed to build scientific research stations there.

Most of Antarctica is protected by the Antarctic Treaty, which was signed by 26 countries in 1961. The treaty states that Antarctica should be used for peaceful purposes and scientific research. Nuclear explosives and dumping of radioactive waste is banned. All scientific research is to be shared with the world's scientists.

In 1991, it was also agreed that no mining could take place there for 50 years. This is called the Environmental Protocol.

Scientific bases have produced waste in Antarctica that spoils the area. Countries have been told to clean up their bases as part of the agreement to care for this pristine environment.

Agreements about children's rights

In 1989, the United Nations made a document about children's rights called the "Convention on the Rights of the Child." The UN asked the world's countries to make the rights of children the law. Nearly every country in the world has agreed to the convention.

The convention says that a child is an individual as well as a member of a family and a community. A child is a human being with the full range of rights regardless of their nationality, skin color, gender, language, religion, and political or social group.

The International Labor Organization (ILO) is one of the UN's agencies concerned with humanitarian issues. It is trying to protect children's rights.

CASE STUDY: An ILO convention to protect children

Not all of the world's children are treated fairly and equally. In some countries, children are forced to go to work before they reach the age of 15. The work may be hard and boring. The pay is usually low and the working conditions can be dangerous and unhealthy.

This is known as child labor. Some children even have to work as slaves, without pay of any kind.

The ILO has made a convention called the "Elimination of the Worst Forms of Child Labor." More than 100 countries have signed ILO Convention Number 182. This support from many of the world's countries shows that they want to make global connections to stop children being exploited for their labor.

GLOBAL FACT
The ILO estimates that in the year 2002, there were nearly 250 million children aged 5 to 17 years in child labor.

Global aid and action

Government foreign aid

foreign aid
help from one country to another by giving money or assistance

interest
the charge on money that is lent to a person or country

Governments are making global connections through their foreign aid projects. They give money, goods, or services as foreign aid. They also lend money that countries have to repay later. Foreign aid money can pay for packages of food, clothing, housing, education, medical services, and farm equipment. Foreign aid does not include military forces, international trade, or money from private companies to set up businesses.

Australia's foreign aid goes through AusAID (Australian Agency for International Development). AusAID is a government agency, based in Canberra. Australia's aid goes mostly to the Pacific and Southeast Asia. Projects range from digging wells in local communities to helping build bridges and telecommunications networks. AusAID also gave money to other aid organizations such as the Red Cross.

In the U.S., the foreign aid department is USAID, based in the city of Washington. USAID has many offices in overseas countries. The staff work with teachers, farmers, entrepreneurs, nurses, and other members of the local communities in Africa, Asia, Europe, South and Central America, the Caribbean, and the Middle East.

Although foreign aid is helping countries, some people believe there are problems. Some of the money given as foreign aid does not reach the local people. There are dishonest governments that have spent millions of dollars in aid money on weapons, their own office buildings, and expensive airports. There is also the problem that poor countries usually cannot afford to repay money loans, especially if interest is added.

This foreign aid worker is helping a villager learn work skills.

What can I do?
AusAID has a great Web site for kids in their "Global Education" section at <www.ausaid.gov.au>. It has lots of case studies about foreign aid. I'm going to use the site to research my latest school project.

Non-government aid

There are organizations separate from governments that make global connections. They are called non-governmental organizations (NGOs). NGOs help make the world a fairer and more sustainable place.

The term "NGOs" was first used at the same time as the United Nations was created in 1945. NGOs are organizations of citizens that work closely with governments. Citizens run NGOs, not governments.

NGOs are important because they:
◎ work with people at the local level
◎ make sure that aid is used effectively in self-help projects
◎ work with the general public to raise donations
◎ help train volunteers.

Many of the NGOs have subgroups within them that get young people involved in the issues. They believe that young people can make a difference, so they encourage them to join the organization as a donor or volunteer. There are even worldwide NGOs run by young people.

There is an Internet community for organizations dealing with human rights and sustainable development worldwide. This is called OneWorld and is at <www.oneworld.net>. OneWorld connects over 1,250 groups working for social justice.

non-governmental organizations (NGOs) citizens' action groups that organize help and spread understanding about global issues

self-help projects projects that are supported by foreign aid for a short period to help a local community become sustainable

social justice fairness for all people

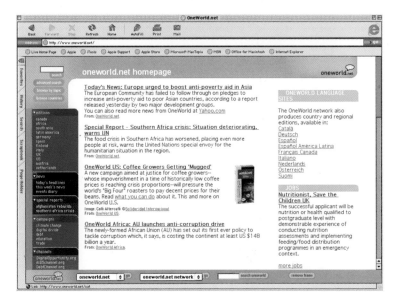

CASE STUDY

The ENYA network is a youth NGO

ENYA (Ecumenical Youth) is an international youth movement of churches and faith communities. The network includes a range of ecumenical and civil groups concerned with peace, human rights, and environmental issues. The network connects 52 countries around the world. ENYA is working with local and international partners to help make a difference in the world.

The work of NGOs

The work that NGOs do covers many global issues. Some NGOs are concerned with environmental issues. Others are concerned about humanitarian issues. Some NGOs cover both broad areas. Groups such as Friends of the Earth, Rainforest Action Network, and The Wilderness Society work for the environment and for human rights. Both issues need to be acted on if planet Earth is to become sustainable.

endangered species
any type of plant or animal that faces a very high risk of dying out

 World Wildlife Fund

The World Wildlife Fund (WWF) is a global conservation NGO. It has five million supporters and 3,330 WWF staff worldwide.

WWF was started in 1961. Since then it has helped over 13,000 projects in 157 different countries. Each year it helps more than 1,200 projects that work towards saving our planet. WWF uses a beautiful panda as its logo to show its promise to try to protect the world's endangered species and wild lands.

There are only 400 to 500 wild Sumatran tigers left. WWF is trying to protect them from extinction.

 Rainforest Action Network

"The mahogany tree or the black leopard beneath the canopy cannot speak in government chambers or corporate boardrooms. It is our responsibility to speak on their behalf as best we can."

This is a statement from the Rainforest Action Network, which was started in 1985. The Rainforest Action Network has been working to protect tropical rain forests and the human rights of indigenous peoples living in and around those forests. Their Web site has a special "Kids Corner" at <www.ran.org/kids_action> that shows how young people can learn about rain forest destruction.

International Red Cross

The International Committee of the Red Cross (ICRC) was founded in 1863. Its aim is to protect the lives and dignity of victims of war and civil violence, and to provide them with assistance. It manages the international relief activities conducted by the Red Cross and Red Crescent in situations of conflict. It also tries to stop suffering by acting for humanitarian values.

The ICRC was responsible for making a set of rules of behavior in war called "international humanitarian law."

These have been agreed to by nearly every nation in the world through an international agreement called the Geneva Convention. Geneva is a city in Switzerland where the founder of the Red Cross, Henry Dunant, was a citizen. Geneva is the headquarters of the ICRC.

A red cross (or red crescent in some countries) on a white background became the symbol of the organization. Those fighting a war could easily see it. Volunteers wearing the symbol expect to be protected from harm as they help victims.

 Oxfam International

Oxfam International is an NGO with a network of member organizations in nine different countries: Oxfam America; Community Aid Abroad, Australia; Oxfam Belgique; Oxfam Canada; Oxfam Hong Kong; Novib, Netherlands; Oxfam New Zealand; Oxfam Quebec; Oxfam United Kingdom, and Ireland.

The NGOs support community-based programs in over 30 countries in areas such as: human rights, the environment, community health, community education, sustainable agriculture, indigenous peoples, and gender.

They work in the belief that self-help is the best way for communities to rise above their problems.

Making global connections

People and organizations all over the world connect to each other every day in a range of ways. These global connections can help us all share in global responsibility. We can all share the responsibility of working towards a fairer and more sustainable world.

We are all citizens of the world. But some of us are more active than others. Some people think that "action" means protesting or doing something violent. But action can take many forms and can always be peaceful, even in a protest march.

Global responsibility through global connections means that global citizens can:

◎ learn to respect life, both in the natural environment and the human world

◎ make decisions about the products we buy

◎ link to organizations that are working to make a difference.

Global citizens can make a difference to global sustainability. Remember: an idea is only an idea until someone puts it into action. We can use global connections to help make a difference to the world's people and environment.

What can we do?

Global citizens discuss global issues to try to find ways of solving them. There is hope for the planet if global citizens act together.

agencies subgroups of a large organization

citizen a person living in a larger group of people who they mix with

citizenship becoming a citizen of a country by being accepted into its nationality

civilian a person who does not belong to any defense forces

conflict violent disagreement

consume to buy things and use them in everyday living

cultural diversity the variety of cultural backgrounds in the world's people

developed countries countries with a high standard of wealth and comfort for most people

developing countries countries with much lower standards of wealth and comfort than developed countries

digital divide the gap between people who use computers and those that do not

ecologically sustainable development (ESD) living in a way that reduces human impact on Earth and helps preserve resources for the future

endangered species any type of plant or animal that faces a very high risk of dying out

environmental issues problems that are about the environment

environments natural and built surroundings

European Union (EU) a group of 15 countries in Europe who have joined together for economic reasons

exploit to use selfishly and for personal gain

foreign aid help from one country to another by giving money or assistance

global warming an overall increase in the world's temperature

greenhouse gases the gases that surround Earth and trap heat near the surface

harmony with a sense of balance

heritage things from the past and present that are valued and saved for future generations

humanitarian issues problems that are about human lives

indigenous peoples groups with the same language and culture who are related to the first people in an area

interest the charge on money that is lent to a person or country

international worldwide

landmines bombs hidden in the earth that explode when stepped on

non-governmental organizations (NGOs) citizens' action groups that organize help and spread understanding about global issues

pristine totally unspoiled by humans

self-help projects projects that are supported by foreign aid for a short period to help a local community become sustainable

slaves people who are owned by another, have no freedom, and must obey the owner

social justice fairness for all people

sustainable to stay strong and last for a long period of time

tariffs extra costs or taxes put on imports from another country, making them more expensive

technology modern equipment and processes

trade the buying and selling of goods and services between different places

transnationals (TNCs) huge companies that have a head office in one country and factories in other countries

treaty an agreement between two or more countries, which they all sign

wealth the amount of money and resources that a country has

Index